Learning My ABC's

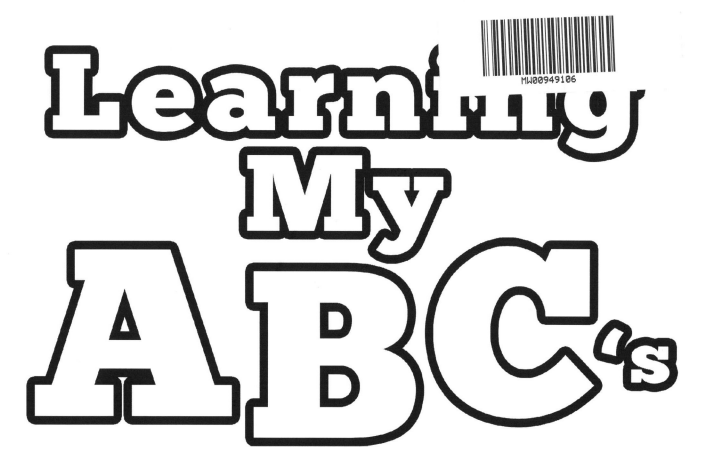

Writing & Coloring Book

Dexter Humphrey

Jasa Leadership Group is an edcuational resource firm that develops products, strategies, and initiaves for students, parents, and academic leaders. Our educational mission: Every student reading and every student learning.

www.JasaLeadership.com

JLG
JASA LEADERSHIP GROUP

This Book Belongs To:

_____

www.LearningMyABCs.com

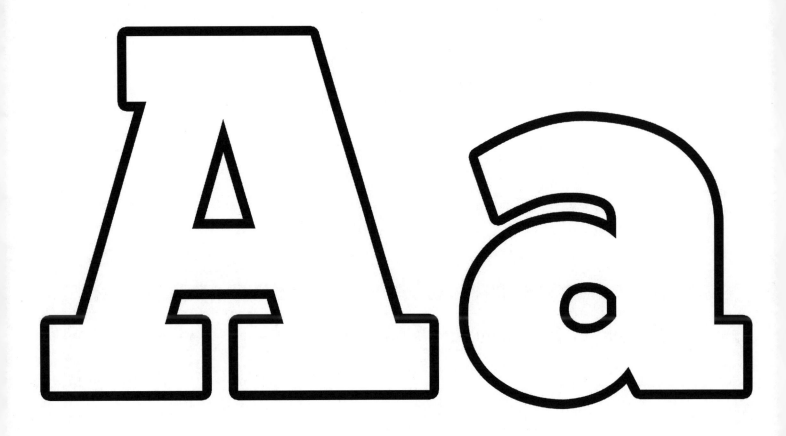

Apple

Bb

B B B B B

b b b b b

Basketball

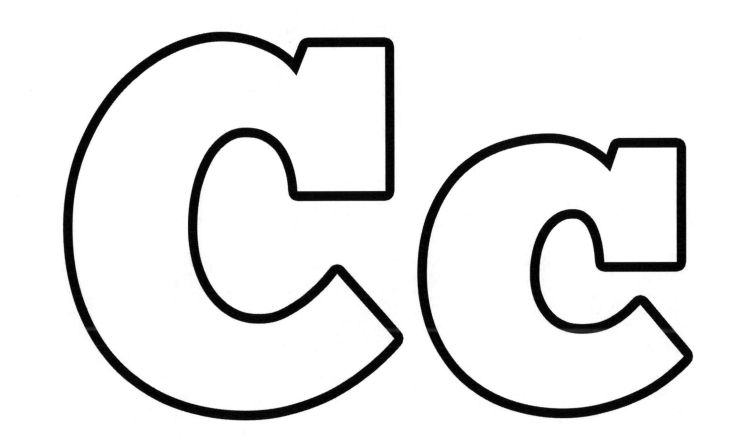

Castle

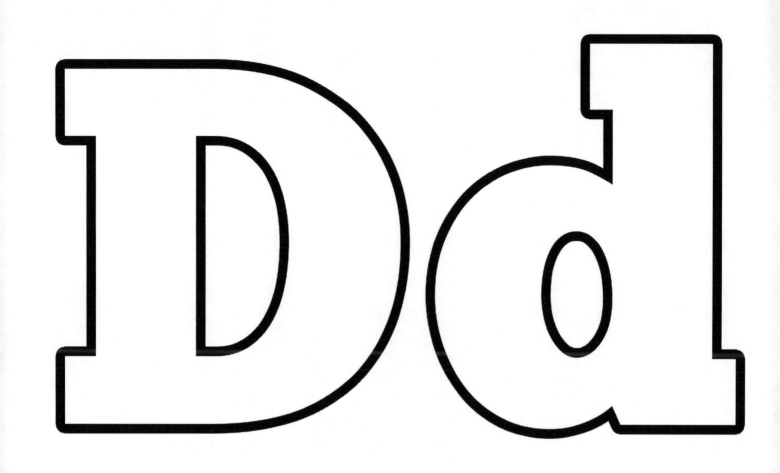

Doggie

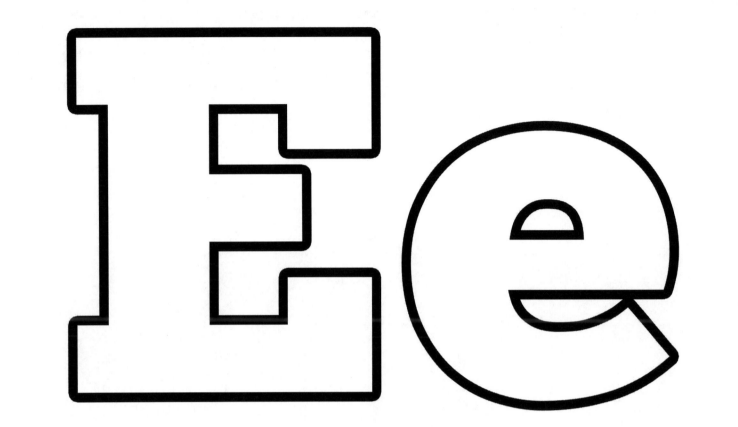

Eagle

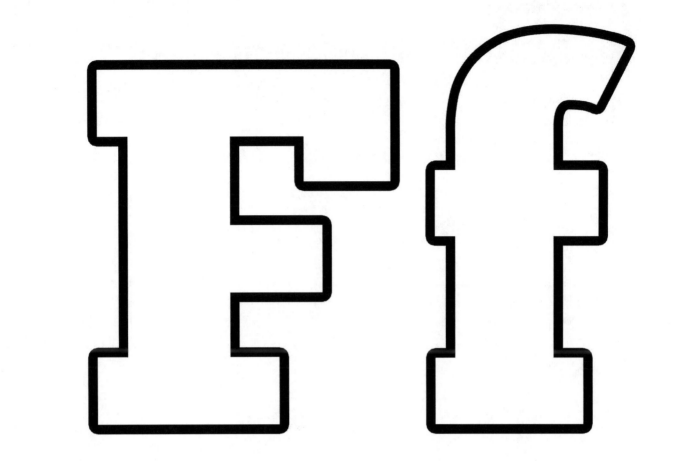

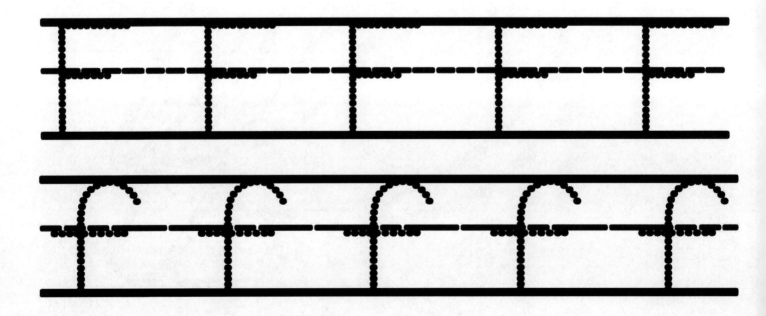

Football

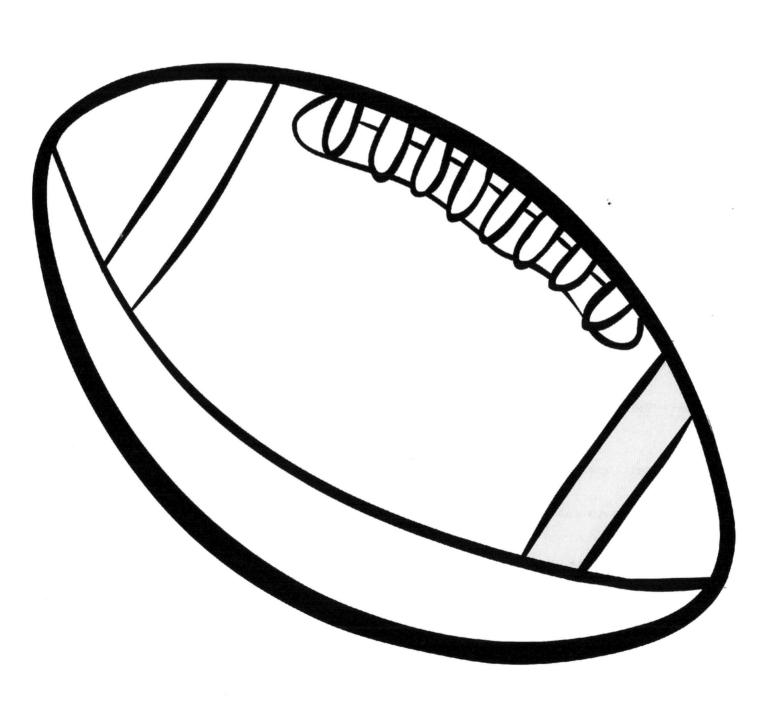

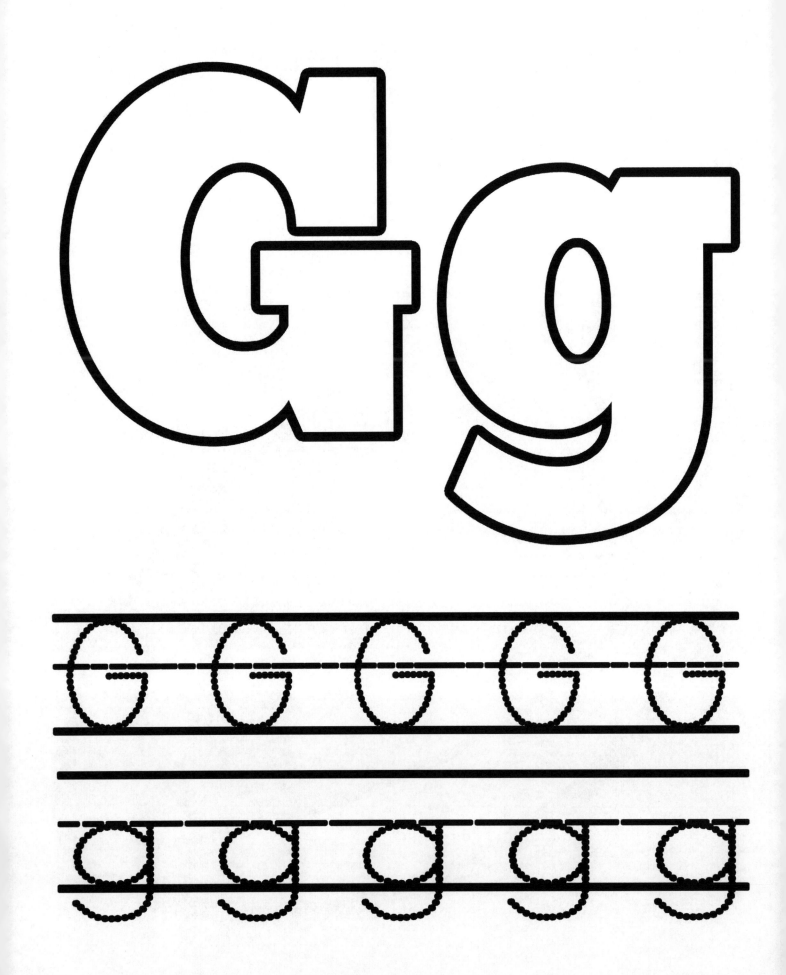

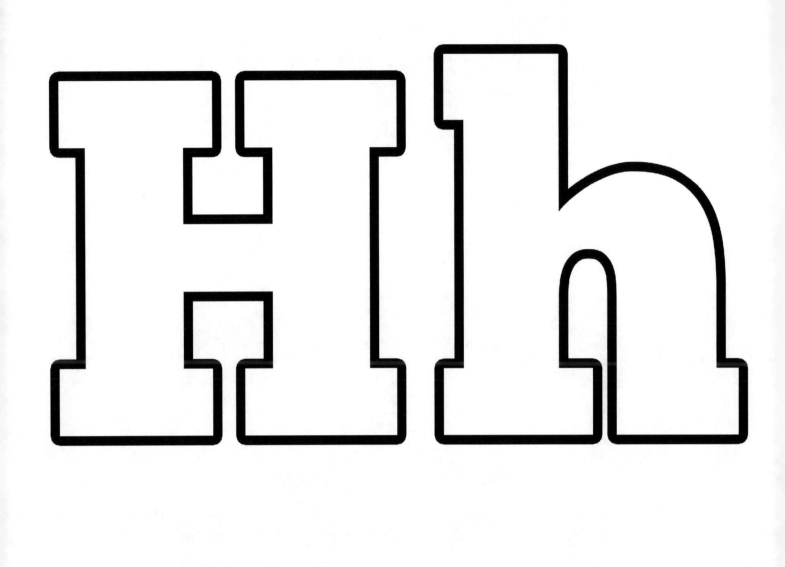

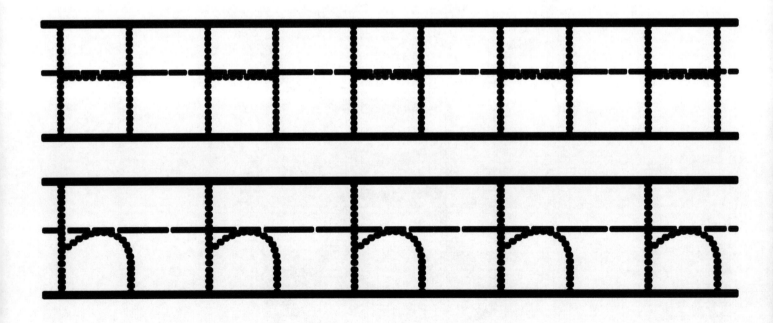

Happy

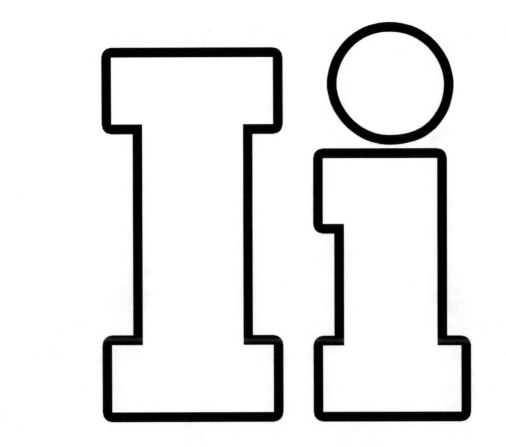

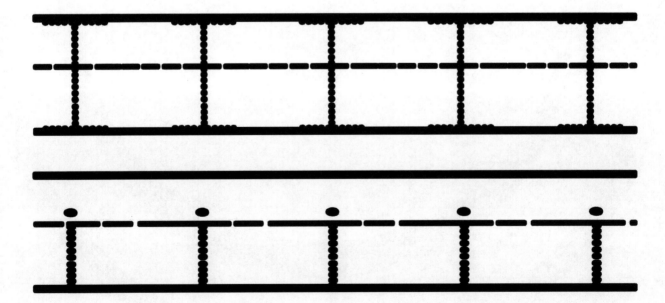

Ice

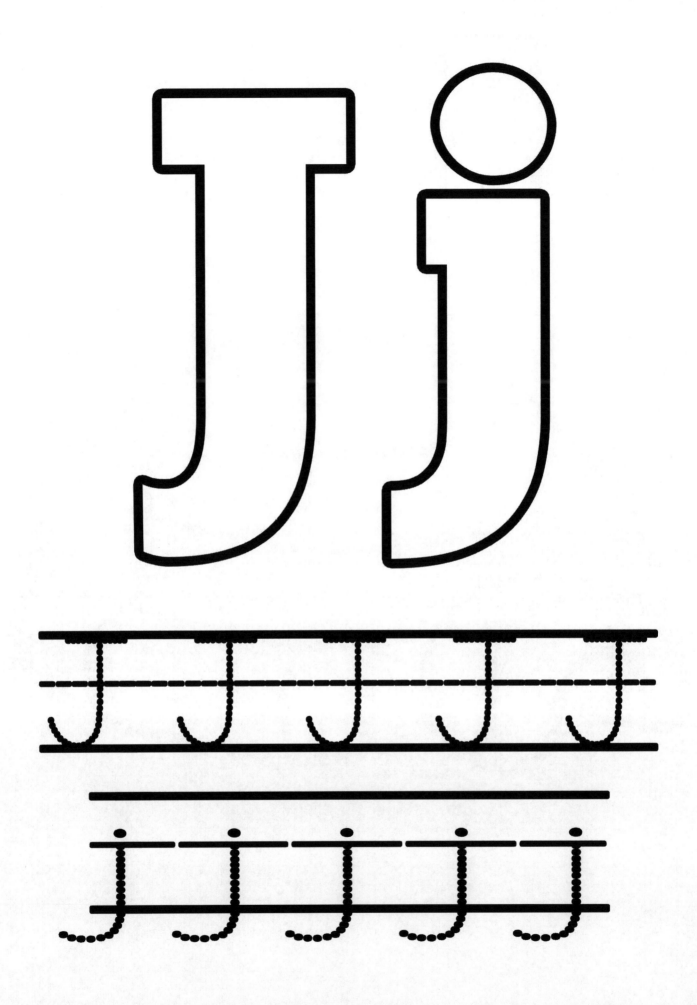

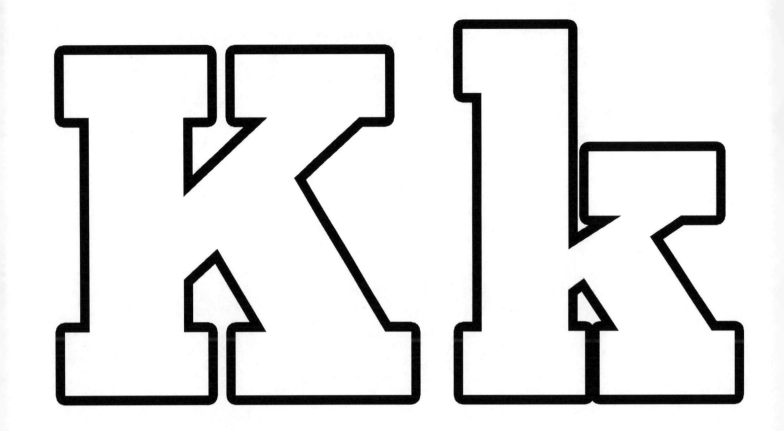

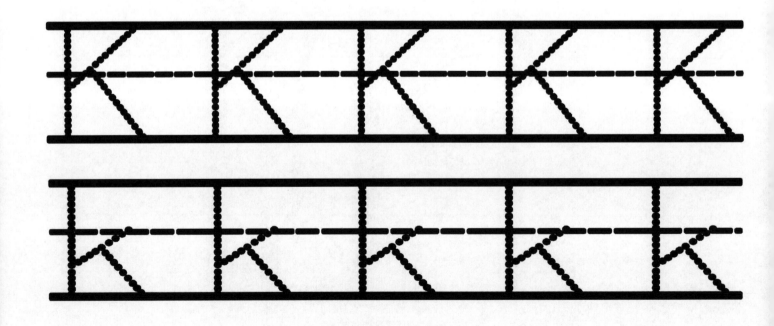

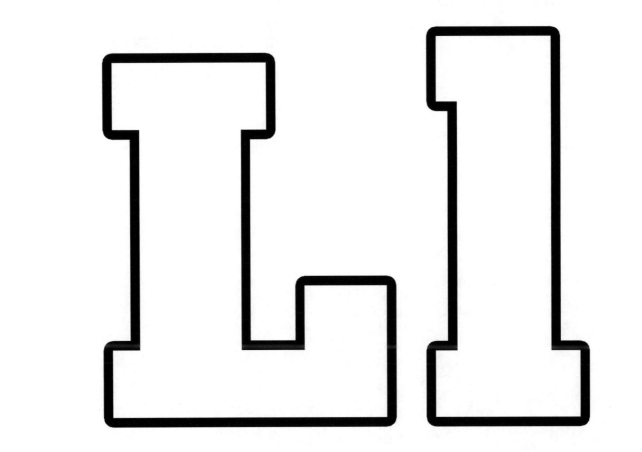

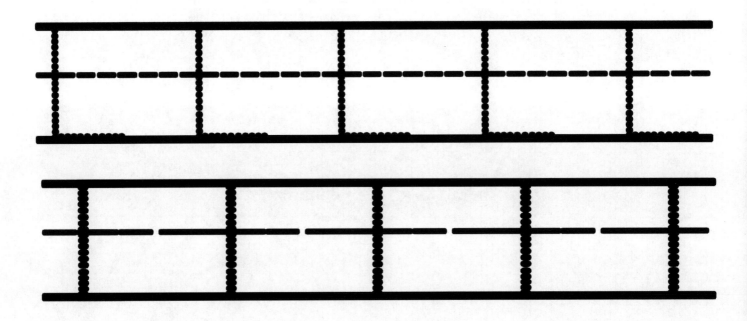

Love

Milkshake

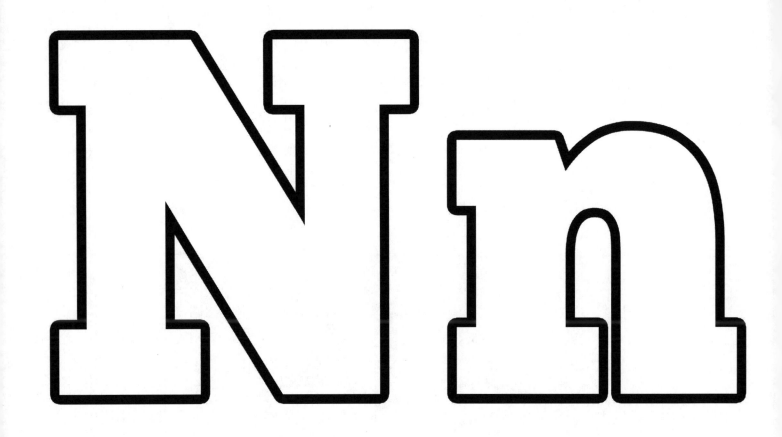

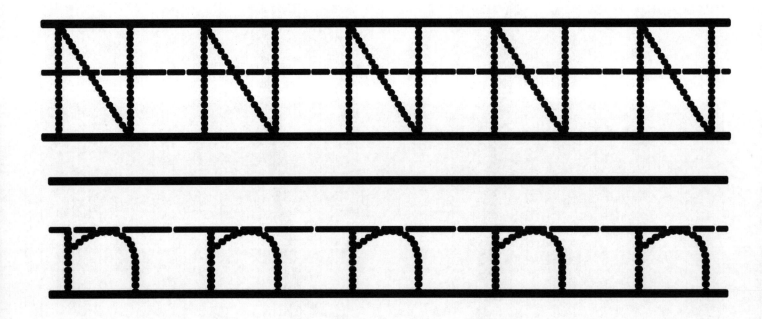

Nails

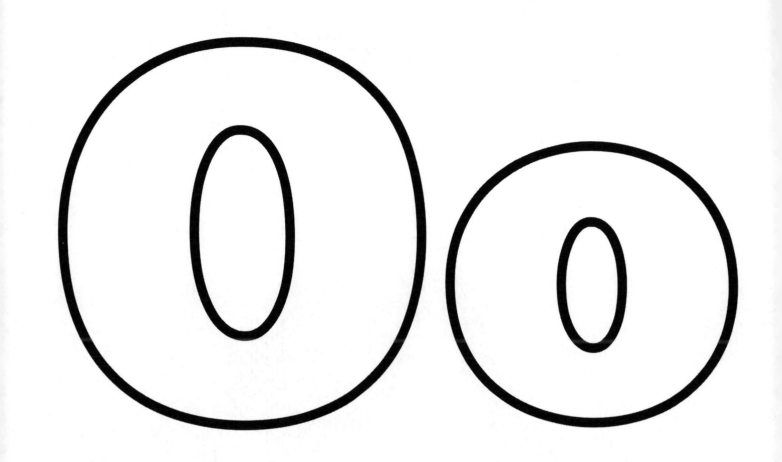

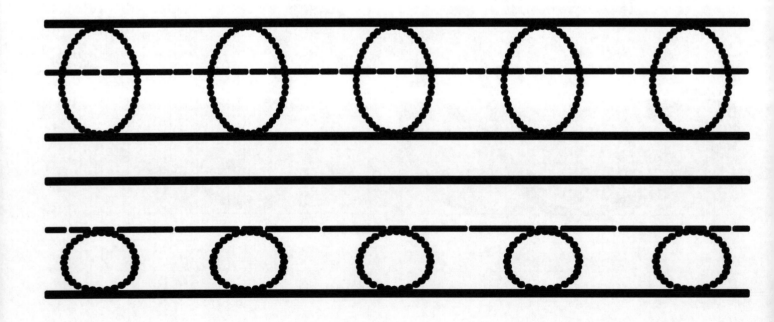

Octopus

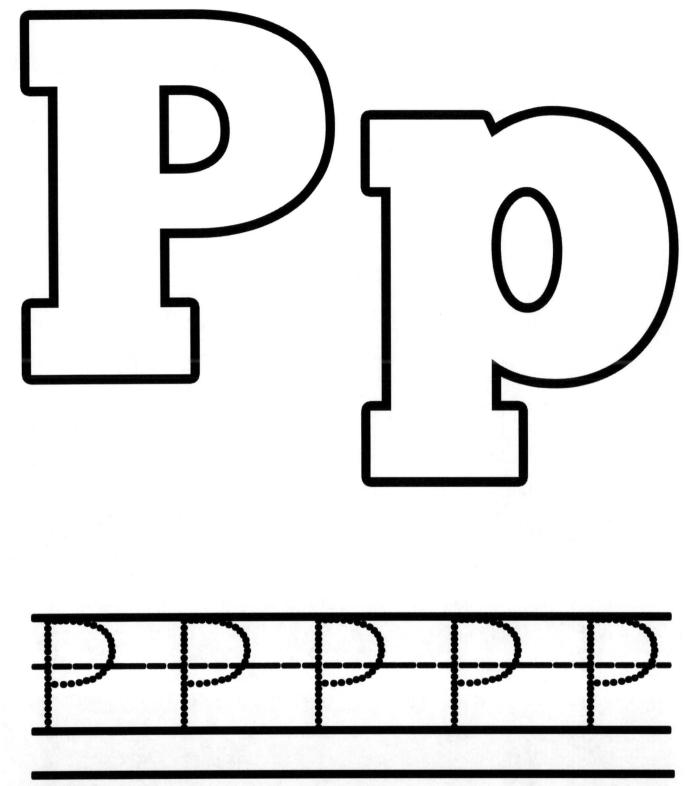

Pencils

Quarter

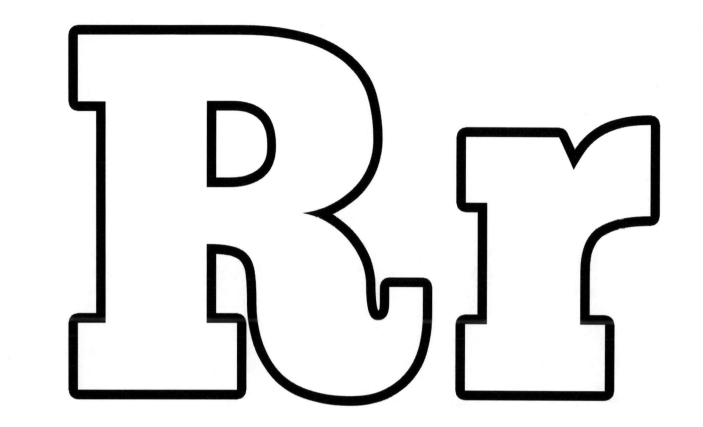

Star

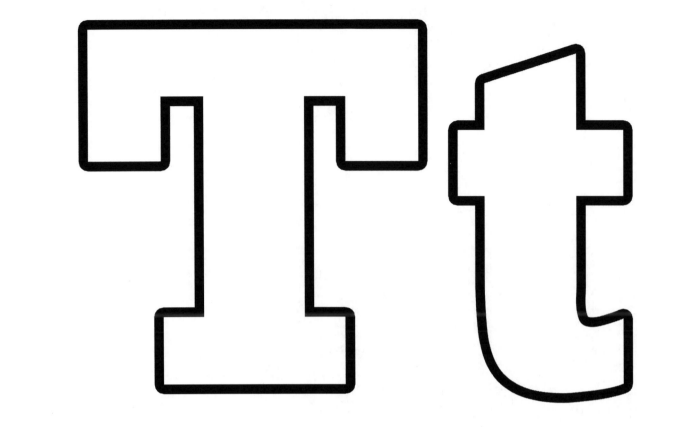

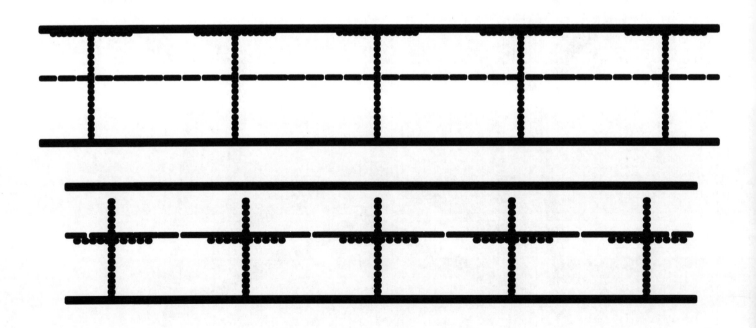

Toys

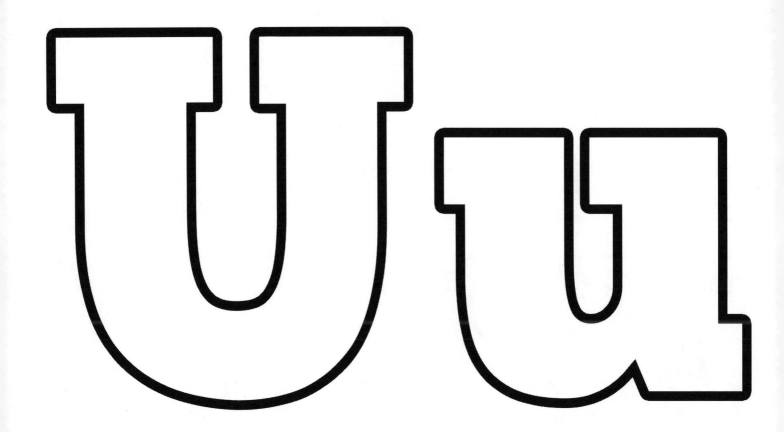

Umbrella

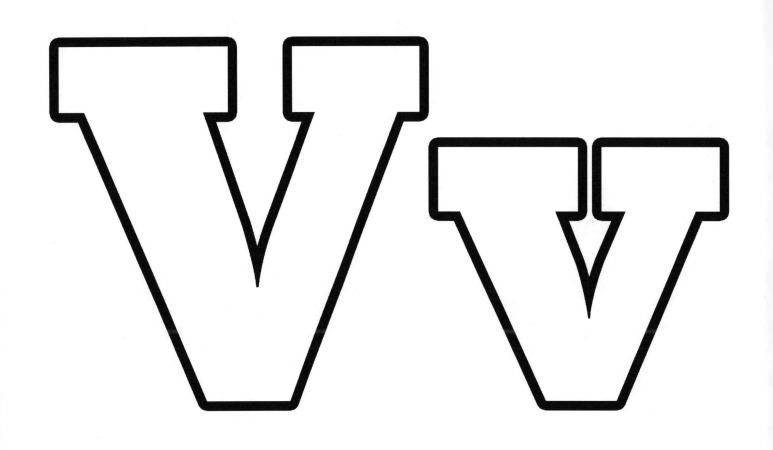

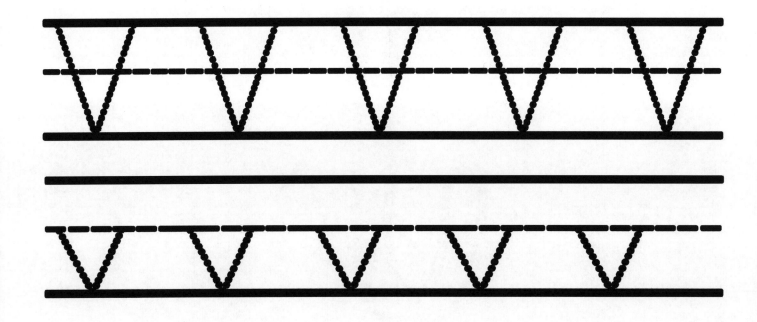

Violin

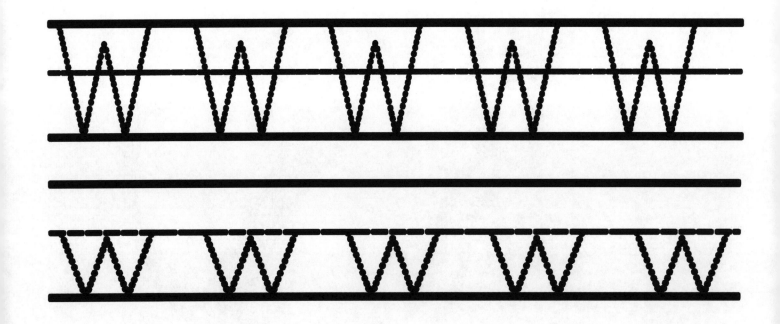

Water

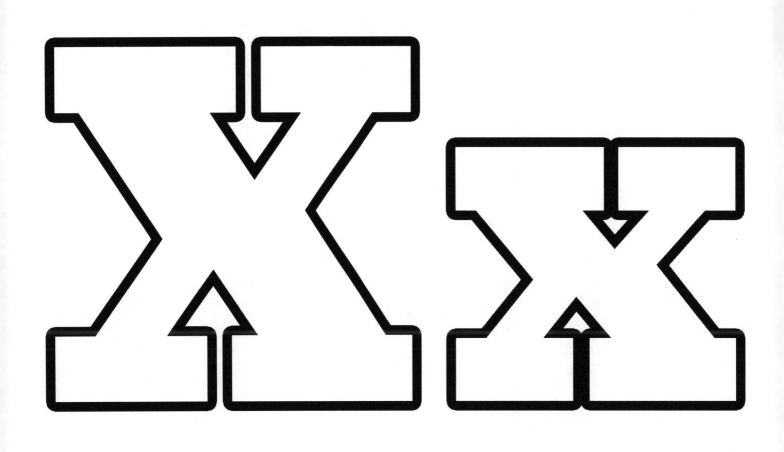

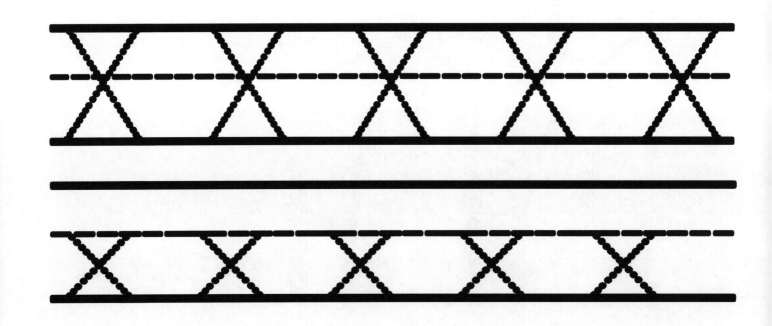

X-ray

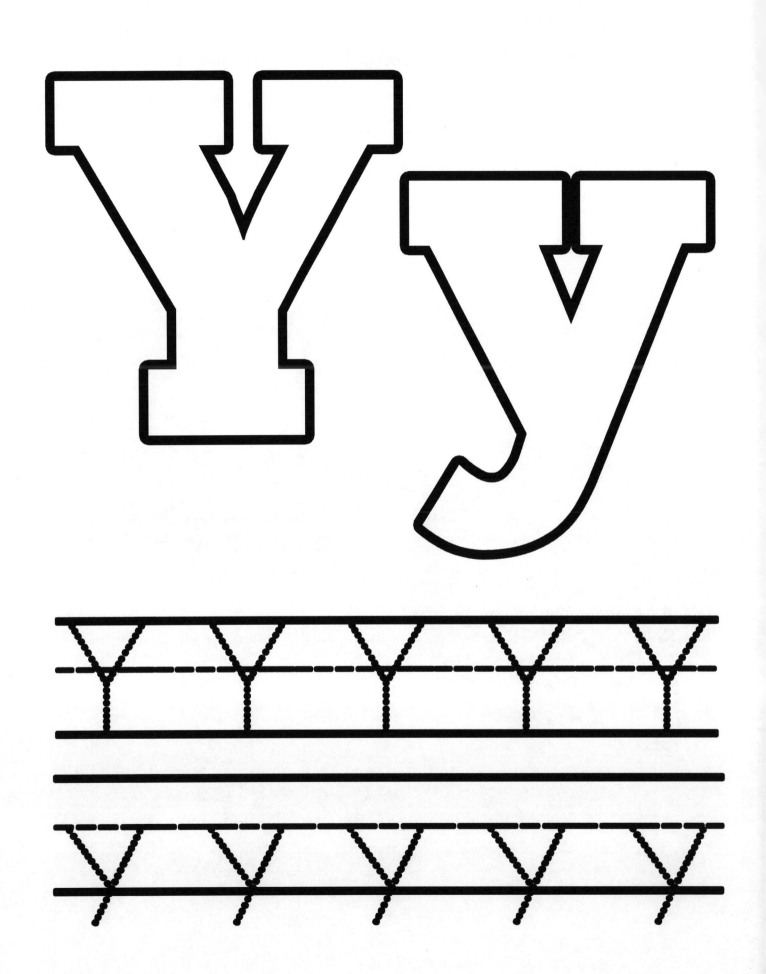

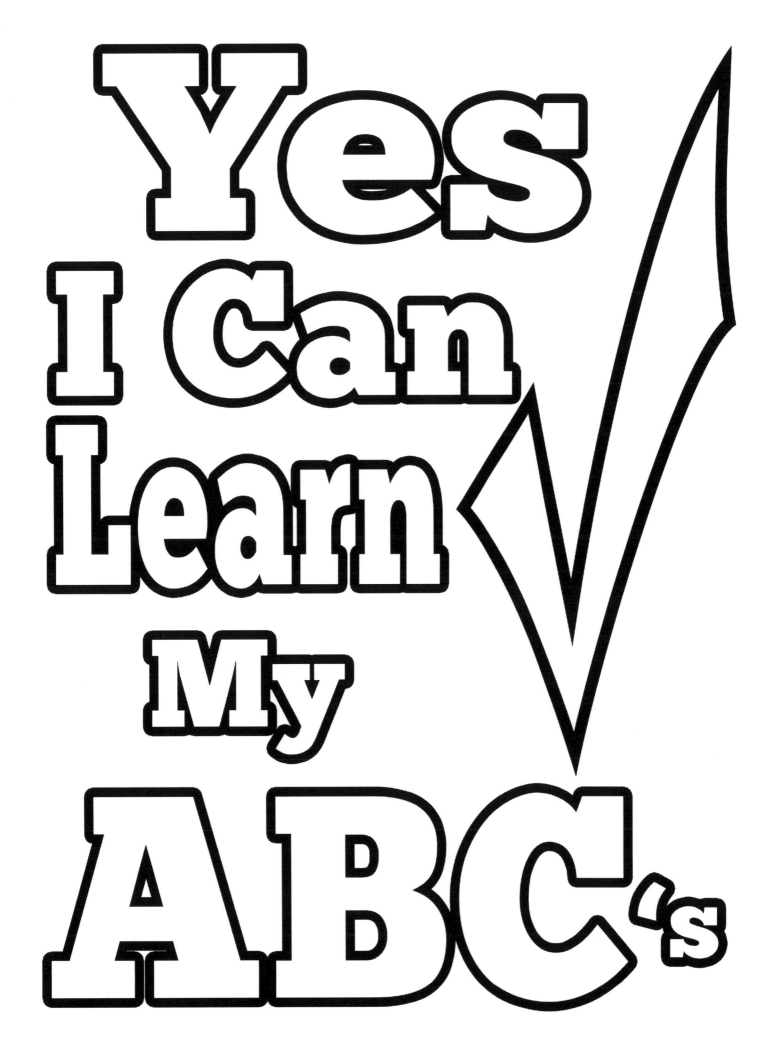

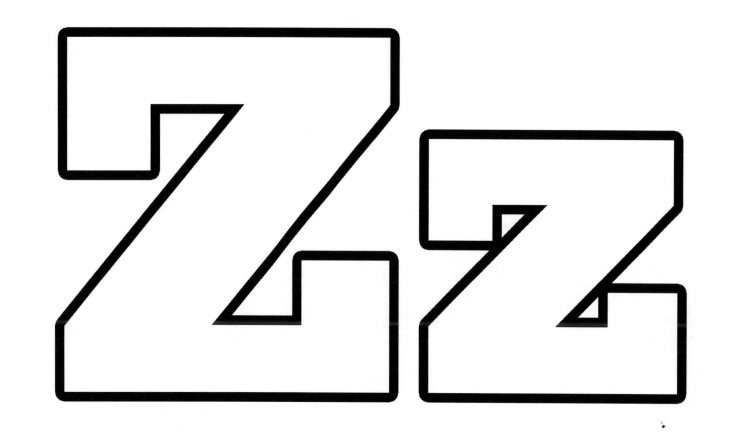

Zoom

Learning My ABC's Literacy System

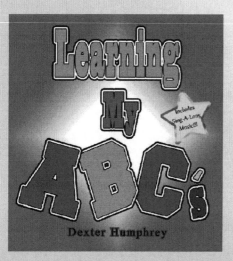

Picture & Music Book

Poster

Flashcards

www.LearningMyABCs.com

Made in the USA
Middletown, DE
04 April 2022

63569977R00033